ON THE JOB
Creative Careers

Be an ANIMATOR!

Jodyanne Benson

PowerKiDS press

Published in 2025 by The Rosen Publishing Group, Inc.
2544 Clinton Street, Buffalo, NY 14224

Copyright © 2025 by The Rosen Publishing Group, Inc.

All rights reserved. No part of this book may be reproduced in any form without permission in writing from the publisher, except by a reviewer.

First Edition

Editor: Theresa Emminizer
Book Design: Michael Flynn

Photo Credits: Cover SeventyFour/Shutterstock.com; (series background) KanokpolTokumhnerd/Shutterstock.com; (series boxes) vector illustration/Shutterstock.com; p. 5 New Africa/Shutterstock.com; p. 7 adriaticfoto/Shutterstock.com; p. 9 Featureflash Photo Agency/Shutterstock.com; p. 11 Frame Stock Footage/Shutterstock.com; p. 13 goodluz/Shutterstock.com; p. 15 MarbellaStudio/Shutterstock.com; p. 17 Michael San Diego/Shutterstock.com; p. 19 Allstar Picture Library Limited/Alamy Stock Photo; p. 21 Gorodenkoff/Shutterstock.com; p. 22 yakub88/Shutterstock.com; p. 23 Andres Conema/Shutterstock.com; p. 25 George Rudy/Shutterstock.com; p. 26 Prostock-studio/Shutterstock.com; p. 27 BearFotos/Shutterstock.com; p. 29 CREATISTA/Shutterstock.com.

Cataloging-in-Publication Data

Names: Benson, Jodyanne.
Title: Be an animator! / Jodyanne Benson.
Description: Buffalo, NY : PowerKids Press, 2025. | Series: On the job: creative careers | Includes glossary and index.
Identifiers: ISBN 9781499449518 (pbk.) | ISBN 9781499449525 (library bound) | ISBN 9781499449532 (ebook)
Subjects: LCSH: Animation (Cinematography)–Vocational guidance–Juvenile literature.
Classification: LCC TR897.5 B46 2025 | DDC 741.5/8023–dc23

Manufactured in the United States of America

Some of the images in this book illustrate individuals who are models. The depictions do not imply actual situations or events.

CPSIA Compliance Information: Batch #CWPK25. For Further Information contact Rosen Publishing at 1-800-237-9932.

CONTENTS

It's Alive! 4
So Much to Do!. 6
Skills and Passion. 8
The Animator's Toolkit. 14
Advanced Tools. 16
Types of Animators 18
Becoming an Animator 24
Plan for Success 28
Glossary 30
For More Information. 31
Index 32

IT'S ALIVE!

Animators bring stories to life. They use computers to make their art move in a lifelike way. Animation can even make images look so real that they appear to be moving right in front of you. This is called three-dimensional (3-D) animation.

Animators are artists who create animations and **visual effects (VFX)**. Sometimes animators are called **multimedia** artists. They use technology to create animated art. This means that they use a machine to make art look like it's moving. Animation uses drawings, computer graphics, or pictures to tell a story. Animators may create storyboards and write scripts. Some animators also help with **designing** backgrounds and organizing projects.

An animation storyboard shows what a scene will look like before it becomes part of a movie or television show.

SO MUCH TO DO!

When animators aren't designing, they're doing a lot of research, or studying. They have a lot to learn in order to make realistic characters. Animators also do a lot of editing. Directors and **clients** give them lots of feedback. This feedback helps animators make sure their work is original and eye-catching. Animators also meet with a lot of people to go over deadlines and talk about projects to come.

For example, more than 600 animators, artists, and **technicians** worked on Disney's *Beauty and the Beast* (1991) over two years. An animation team also came up with the ideas for *A Bug's Life* (1998), *Monsters, Inc.* (2001), *Finding Nemo* (2003), and *WALL-E* (2008) during a lunchtime brainstorming meeting in 1994.

Animators often work with a team of talented, artistic people.

SKILLS AND PASSION

Animators need to be creative and love small details. They also need technical skills. This means they need to mix their artistic skills, such as drawing, with **practical** skills such as using software, or computer programs that do certain tasks. A lot of animators have a great sense of humor! They watch how people move and talk. This helps them create interesting characters.

There are many types of animators. Animators usually choose a specific type of art to work with. Some work on animation or visual effects for movies and television shows. Others work on video games or commercials. Animators also create scenes or backgrounds. Knowing your skills and passions will help you find the right career path as an animator.

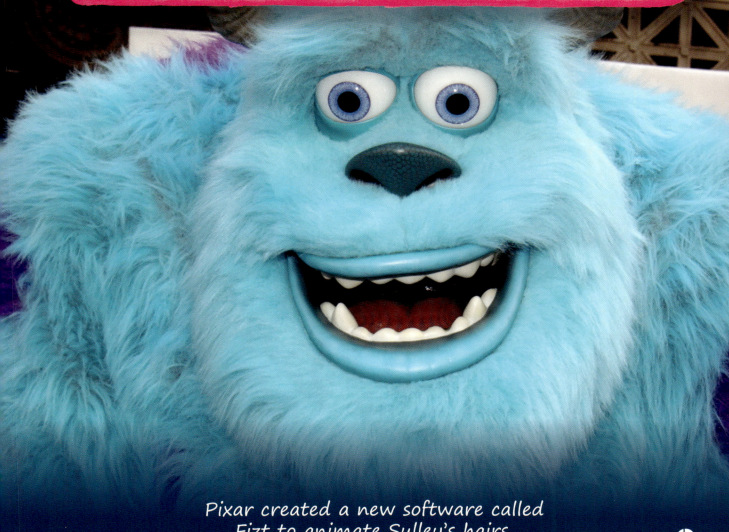

LEARNING ON THE JOB!

Sulley from Monsters, Inc. has more than 2.3 million hairs. A single **frame** of the monster took about 12 hours to create because of his detail.

Pixar created a new software called Fizt to animate Sulley's hairs.

Animators have many unique, or one-of-a-kind, skills. It takes more than drawing on a computer to make a character come alive! Animators need both artistic and technical skills.

Technology has made it possible for animators to make characters and stories seem even more alive. Many animators go to a college or technical school to learn important skills. Special programs teach animators technical skills like audio and video editing. They also practice using software programs like Adobe Animate, Adobe After Effects, Premiere Pro, and Cinema 4D. Additionally, animators must be able to learn software programs on their own. New software is always being created.

Audio and video editing is usually done at the end of a project. It can include color correction and sound mixing.

Animators take classes in graphic design and motion. These classes teach future animators how to create figures. They also learn about timing and spacing movement to make their characters realistic. Spacing is the placement of objects in an animation's different frames.

Animators are also very creative and artistic. They have strong drawing skills. They also never stop learning about art. For example, animators study color and how color can express different feelings. An animator's drawings help other people visualize, or picture, an idea.

Animators also appreciate small details and love to observe the world. They notice people's expressions and movements. These observations help them draw realistically.

LEARNING ON THE JOB!

Animators for the movie How to Train Your Dragon (2010) went to flight school to learn about how creatures really move in the air.

Motion graphics classes teach a wide range of concepts—from learning about colors to using animation software.

THE ANIMATOR'S TOOLKIT

A beginner animator usually starts with a stylus pen and graphics tablet. A stylus pen lets you draw on a computer tablet. Getting used to the tablet as your drawing space takes a lot of practice. It will feel much different than drawing on paper. But this is where a lot of animation begins.

Once you're ready for animating your art, you'll need a computer software program such as Adobe Animate. Drawings from a tablet can be easily moved from the tablet to these programs. This is where the real animation work starts!

LEARNING ON THE JOB!

The Lego Movie (2014) began with a Lego building software called LEGO Digital Designer that anyone can use.

Animators can find it easier to draw with a stylus than with a computer mouse.

ADVANCED TOOLS

Animators also use advanced tools like 3-D animation software. This software allows animators to play with modeling. Modeling is how a 3-D **representation** of a real-life object gets made. It's like what builders do when they construct something. This is an important part of animation.

Three-dimensional software also helps create realistic animals for movies. However, no matter how advanced these programs become, they can't completely replace an animator's drawing ability.

> In the 1990s, Toy Story was the first full-length feature film that was entirely 3-D computer animated.

Animation Technology Through the Years

1832	Joseph Plateau discovers the first animation tool called the phenakistoscope. A phenakistoscope is a spinning cardboard disk that makes figures look like they are moving when viewed in a mirror.
1914–1967	Animation is drawn by hand on transparent, or clear, plastic sheets and called cel (short for **celluloid**) animations.
1967–1984	Animation of 2-D characters is done completely on computers.
1984–2018	Computer-generated imagery (CGI) begins to be used in animation. Pixar's *Toy Story* (1995) is the first feature-length movie made entirely by CGI technology.
2018–today	Virtual reality and 360-degree video technology become more popular.

TYPES OF ANIMATORS

Animation styles continue to change. Most animators can use different styles, but they usually have a particular style they use the most in their career.

Two-dimensional (2-D) animation is when characters and scenes are created in 2-D space. This means that they have length and width but no thickness. Computers are used to create digital animations that can be **manipulated** easily. Successful animators can use a lot of different tools and software.

Animators who use 2-D styles work in many different fields. They make cartoons for television shows, anime, and even video games. Some animators are making 2-D video games that are as popular as 3-D games.

LEARNING ON THE JOB!

Around 350,000 drawings were made for Disney's Robin Hood (1973). There were also more than 100,000 painted cels and 800 painted backgrounds.

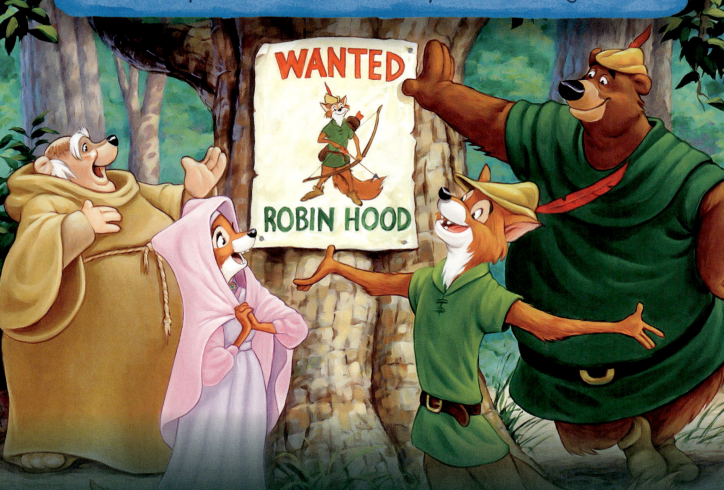

Cel drawing animation involves drawing outlines on one side of a cel, adding colors to the other side, and then placing both sides over a background.

Three-dimensional animation uses computer programs to create characters and scenes. This kind of animation seems more lifelike because the objects have length, width, and thickness. The technique to create it is called computer-generated imagery (CGI). It is different than traditional animation that uses hand-drawn characters. Three-dimensional animators know how to model a character on the computer, shape it, and give it a skeleton that can be moved around.

Today, 3-D animation is used for more than just creating movies. Medicine, interior design, and architecture, or building design, all use 3-D animation technology. But this kind of technology can be very difficult to work with. So, 3-D animators take classes and practice with trained **professionals**.

LEARNING ON THE JOB!

Computer-generated imagery (CGI) helped the animators of Disney's Aladdin (1992) create the magic carpet ride through the Cave of Wonders.

Computer generated (CG) animation transformed, or changed, actor Andy Serkis on screen into a creature called Gollum in the Lord of the Rings movies.

Stop-motion is a technique that puts a character or object against a background. Then, a picture is taken to create a frame. The character or object is slightly changed before making another frame. It is similar to 2-D animation. Stop motion tricks the eye into seeing movement. Clay animation, also called Claymation, uses the same steps as stop motion. But plasticine, or clay, is used for the characters, objects, and scenes.

Professional animators learn and practice many different animation styles. The great animators know the history of animation and the styles that have changed over time. They can be inspired by any of these styles. Each style tells a story in a special way.

Tim Burton

Tim Burton's The Nightmare Before Christmas made stop-motion animation popular again in 1993 even after computer generated animation had taken off.

Becoming an Animator

If you love art and technology, then it might be time to start exploring a career in animation. Animation takes learning and practice. Are you ready to begin your journey to becoming an animator? Let's get started!

Animators share many similar characteristics, or traits. They are creative and imaginative. They also love to think about the world in new and exciting ways. Patience and attention to detail are important qualities for animators. Sometimes animators need to edit or re-create their designs over and over again to get them right. This process can take a lot of time and energy.

LEARNING ON THE JOB!

An animation of 60 seconds can take around eight to ten weeks to create. The time frame depends on the type of animation, such as if it's 2-D or 3-D.

Sometimes animators are born with a lot of talent for creating and drawing. But they also work very hard to learn animation skills.

Animators communicate well with others. It's important for animators to be able to help others see a possible idea for a character or story. This makes other people excited to make it a reality.

Animators are able to follow directions and complete their work on time. Animation also needs good teamwork. There can be anywhere from two to hundreds of people working on a project! Animators are good at working both alone and with others.

Have you ever heard someone tell you that practice makes perfect? This is really important when it comes to animation. Animation is **competitive** and challenging. Practice drawing and keep learning!

Even if animators aren't great with computers in the beginning, they can learn how to become better. They can take classes, ask questions, and practice with teachers.

PLAN FOR SUCCESS

Most animators go to college or technical school after high school. Animation jobs usually require a college degree in animation, fine arts, or computer graphics. The right animation program for you will depend on your skills and the kind of job you want.

Start building a **portfolio** of your work. Many school programs will help you. You can start replacing old projects with your new work as your skills get stronger.

Finally, get a lot of work experience. You can start learning about jobs and meeting professional animators while you are still in school. This is called networking. If you have an animation idea, start asking your teacher or parents how they can help you get started.

LEARNING ON THE JOB!

Disney assigned less experienced animators to make The Lion King (1994) because nobody believed that the film would become popular.

Many animators take art and acting classes. Acting classes can help you learn more about body movements and feelings to create lifelike characters.

GLOSSARY

celluloid: A transparent sheet of plastic once used in the film industry.

client: A person or business who pays for a professional's service.

competitive: Having to do with an event in which people try to beat others.

design: To create the plans that show how something will be made.

frame: A single still image that makes up a sequence of images. When shown in a fast succession, multiple frames create the illusion of motion.

manipulate: To make changes to something.

multimedia: Using, involving, or encompassing several media, such as video, printed text, animation, etc.

portfolio: A selection of a student's or artist's work collected over a period of time and stored in an album or folder.

practical: Relating to action and practice rather than ideas or thought.

professional: Having to do with a job someone does for a living.

representation: An image that is created to look like a particular thing or person.

technician: Someone who uses machines.

visual effects (VFX): Images created by a computer combined with live action footage to make scenes interesting to an audience.

FOR MORE INFORMATION

BOOKS

Dickmann, Nancy. *Computer Animation*. Buffalo, NY: Kidhaven, 2023.

Gardner, Tracy A., and Elbrie De Kock. *Animation and Stories with ScratchJr*. Buffalo, NY: PowerKids Press, 2021.

Miller, Shannon McClintock, and Blake Hoena. *A Stop-Motion Animation Mission*. Mankato, MN: Stone Arch Books, 2020.

WEBSITES

Make an Animation
www.abcya.com/games/animate
Learn how to make an animation of your own on this ABCya website.

Walt Disney Animation Studios: Technology
www.disneyanimation.com
The Walt Disney Animation Studios website lets you explore Disney projects, technology, and careers.

Publisher's note to educators and parents: Our editors have carefully reviewed these websites to ensure that they are suitable for students. Many websites change frequently, however, and we cannot guarantee that a site's future contents will continue to meet our high standards of quality and educational value. Be advised that students should be closely supervised whenever they access the internet.

INDEX

A
art, 12, 14, 24, 29

B
backgrounds, 4, 19, 22
Burton, Tim, 22, 23

C
characters, 6, 8, 10, 12, 17, 18, 20, 22, 26, 29
Claymation, 22
college, 10, 28
colors, 12, 13, 19
computer-generated imagery (CGI), 17, 20, 21
computer graphics, 4, 28

D
deadlines, 6
Disney, 6, 19
drawing, 8, 10, 12, 14, 16, 19, 25, 26

G
graphics tablet, 14

M
modeling, 16
movement, 12, 22
movies, 5, 13, 14, 16, 17, 20, 21

P
Pixar, 9, 17

S
software, 8, 10, 13, 14, 16, 18
spacing, 12
stop-motion, 22, 23
storyboard, 4, 5
stylus pen, 14

T
teams, 6, 7, 26
three-dimensional (3-D) animation, 4, 16, 20, 25
traits, 24
two-dimensional (2-D) animation, 17, 18, 22, 25